Empowered to Lead

Video-based Learning for
Small Group Facilitators

Joel Comiskey

JOEL COMISKEY
GROUP RESOURCING THE WORLDWIDE CELL CHURCH

Published by CCS Publishing
23890 BrittlebushCircle
Moreno Valley, CA 92557 USA
1-888-511-9995

Cover design by Jason Klanderud

ISBN: 978-1-950069-08-8

CCS Publishing is the book-publishing division of Joel Comiskey Group, a resource and coaching ministry dedicated to equipping leaders for cell-based ministry.

Find us on the World Wide Web at www.joelcomiskeygroup.com

CONTENTS

Going Beyond the Small Group's Name

WATCH THIS VIDEO ▶

https://youtu.be/enTZuNn5UbA

One controversial topic in small group circles is what to call the group. Some resist the word *cell* saying, "It sounds too much like a communistic group." Others do not like the *small group* because it sounds too generic and might include Sunday school classes, choirs, board of elders, and so forth. Others call their groups *Life Groups*, *Heart Groups*, and so on. The names greatly vary.

My conviction is this: the group's name is not as important as the definition of the group.

Most churches worldwide call their groups *cell groups* because David Cho, founder, and pastor of Yoido Full Gospel Church in South Korea, first used this term to describe his groups. He liked the idea of cells in the human body that were constantly multiplying yet stayed within the body. He believed that the cells should connect to the local church structure. And since his church grew to become the largest church in the history of Christianity, the name caught on.

I believe the definition of the group is the most critical aspect of the small group system. If a pastor or leader fails here, the entire structure can crumble or become irrelevant. For example, some churches define their groups so broadly that those groups lose their value. In other words, if everything is a small group, nothing is a small group.

As I've researched small group churches around the world, here's the definition that describes small holistic groups around the world: *small groups of 3 to 15 people who meet weekly outside the church building for the purpose of evangelism, community, and spiritual growth with the goal of making disciples who make disciples that results in multiplication.*

Let's look at this definition step by step.

3-15 people: We're talking about small groups, not large ones. Researchers have found that when the group goes beyond fifteen, it becomes a congregation. The shy person does not have the liberty to speak when the group is over 15 people. Only the extroverts are bold enough to speak out. Churches should avoid this scenario.

When referring to 3-15 people, I am referring to adults. If the small group has children, they can be present with the adults for the icebreaker and worship and then break into groups in another room. The adults can rotate in facilitating the lesson. I recommend that two adults lead the children's slot. Some churches want the children to meet separately for the entire meeting, including icebreaker and worship. In my book *Children in Cell Ministry*, I lay out the different strategies for children and small groups.

On the lower end, the minimum size is three people. Ralph Neighbor once said, "Community starts with three and ends with fifteen." Neighbor cites the Trinity as his example. Two people work well for personal interaction, coaching, or counseling but not community. Group community begins at three.

Fifteen is the higher-end number because more than fifteen diminishes intimacy. The early house churches were small and intimate. As I researched the early house churches for my book *Biblical Foundations for the Cell-based Church*, I discovered that approximately ten people could fit in the early house churches. Twenty was the maximum. Yes, there were exceptions, like the upper room in Acts 2, but most dwelling places were apartment size homes in the city's poor, overcrowded areas.

Weekly groups: I promote weekly groups because frequency enhances quality. I do understand that not everyone will attend each week, but at least people could attend. Groups that meet every other week or once per month find it harder to disciple the members. Jim Egli and Dwight Marable's book *Small Groups; Big Impact* describes this aspect of frequency. They discovered that weekly groups were healthier.

Outside the church building: Small groups penetrate the community and reach out to people where they live and work. It's not a come-and-see event. The building does have an important place. People worship in the building. They often are taught via Sunday school, along with other events. While the building has its place, the focus of small group ministry is to meet where people live, work, and assemble. Small groups often meet in the home, but this is not always the case. Some groups might gather on a university campus, in a park, or garage. Some might get together in a quiet restaurant.

For the purpose of evangelism. Small groups exist for others. They breathe the life of outreach and grow in quality as they reach out. New people bring new vitality to the group. In our book *Groups that Thrive,* Jim Egli and I discovered that evangelistic groups were far more qualitative and intimate than those that closed their doors to outsiders. We also know that the early church houses reached a lost world for Jesus.

Community. People long for a spiritual family. Everyone needs a sense of belonging. Sitting in a pew on Sunday is insufficient and usually very impersonal. We need to be known for who we are and how we feel. So many today are searching for authentic community, and they are not finding it in the church as we know it. Intimate small groups in our study were also more effective in reaching out to others.

Spiritual growth. Small groups should not be a morbid, serious endeavor. Joy and fun should characterize them. Why? Because as people enjoy each other, laughter and friendship flow naturally. Yet, small groups are far more than just having a good time. The members should also hold each other accountable. They realize that time is short on this earth. God desires that each person grows into Christ's likeness, and God uses other believers to fulfill this purpose.

With the goal of making disciples who make disciples. Discipleship is the goal of the small group. Christ's great commission is for the church throughout the ages. Jesus said to his twelve, "All authority in heaven and on earth has been given to me. Therefore, go and make disciples of all nations, baptizing them in the name of the Father and of the Son and of the Holy Spirit" (Matthew 28:18-19). When he said these words, he spoke to the small group he walked with for three years. Jesus made disciples in this group and sent his disciples into the home (Luke 8-9). The early church followed this strategy as they met from house to house (Acts 2:42-46; 5:20; 20:20).

That results in multiplication. Previously, I thought that multiplication was the primary goal of the small group. I taught that groups had to multiply after a specific time, like one year. My thinking caused me to multiply some groups before they were ready. Many of those new multiplications closed because they simply were not strong. I have since changed my thinking.

I now believe that the main goal is to make disciples who make disciples. The result is multiplication. We should not multiply cell groups until disciples are formed and ready to start new spiritual families. Otherwise, we might post large multiplication numbers one year, followed by closed groups and discouraged leaders the following year.

The name of the small group is far less important than the definition. Life groups, small groups, heart groups, or any other name is acceptable. But we must not compromise the quality definition of the group because it is the heart of the small group-based church. Holistic small groups form the base of healthy small group-based churches, and we need to make sure that we start with a healthy, God-honoring definition.

Reflection Questions

What did you learn from this lesson?

How will the lesson's content change or add to your small group definition?

What is the one aspect of the definition that you need to work on the most?

Suggested Reading

Books

- chapter 7 of *Reap the Harvest: How a small group system can grow your church*
- chapter 6 of *Myths and Truths of the Cell Church: Key Principles that Make-or-Break Cell Ministry*
- chapter 2 of *From 12 to 3: How to Apply G-12 Principles in Your Church*

Internet articles (available at www.joelcomiskeygroup.com/resources)

What is a Cell Group?
Holistic Small Groups—What Are They?
What Should You Call Your Groups?
Semester Cells? (should cells take a break)

Why Meet Weekly, Outside the Building?
Online Cells Versus Cells in Person
The Church Next Door
Reasons for Outside the Church Building
Don't Try to Save Time by Calling Everything a Cell
Clearly Defined Cells Make More and Better Disciples
Every House a Church; Every Christian a Minister
Long Term Versus Short Term Success in Cell Ministry
What's the Big Deal about Small Groups?
Family Cells Versus Gender-Specific Cell
Homogeneous Cells in the Cell Church
Seeing the Cell as the Church
More than Fellowship

Download this PowerPoint

Joel Comiskey's PowerPoint on this lesson:

https://www.dropbox.com/s/6ozen1z2ylex9ci/lesson1-definition.pptx?dl=0

The Order of the Small Group Meeting: Introducing the 4Ws

WATCH THIS VIDEO ▶

https://youtu.be/GMI_oZro37M

I remember interviewing a fruitful small group leader who had multiplied her group on several occasions. She mentioned that one of the key reasons for her fruitfulness was that she varied the weekly meetings. She said to me, "Variety is the spice of life."

I was impressed by her flexibility and that she wanted to listen to the Holy Spirit and receive his guidance. Yet, I always tell leaders that it is crucial to have a plan, even though they might not follow the order precisely. Someone said that those who fail to plan, plan to fail.

So, what is an excellent order to follow? I recommend an order called "The 4Ws." I did not create the 4Ws. Ralph Neighbor, an early cell church pioneer, invented it. I like it because it increases participation and leads toward transformation. The 4Ws consist of Welcome, Worship, Word, and Witness.

Welcome. The Welcome time typically starts with an Icebreaker, a thought-provoking question that allows members to know each other. The phrase *Us to Each Other*, describes the Welcome time. The Welcome time usually lasts .15 minutes.

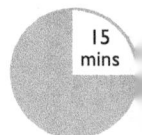

15
mins

Worship. Worship is *Us to God.* This time typically lasts .20 minutes.

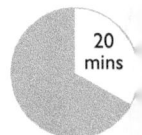

20
mins

Word. *God is speaking to us.* The Word time lasts about .40 minutes, and prayer often follows.

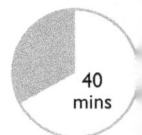

40
mins

Witness. *God is speaking through us to others.* This time typically lasts for .15 minutes.

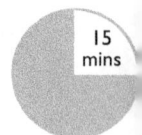

15
mins

I teach that the small group should not be more than 1.5 hours. Some small groups, like the ones in South Korea, last for only one hour.

After 1.5 hours, those present might stay for refreshments for .30 minutes or so. Some groups like to begin with a meal. But it's essential to be sensitive to the host and remember that small group ministry is ongoing. The goal is for people to come back each week.

Let's look at the 4Ws in more detail.

The **Welcome** time should be fun. Often leaders make the mistake of turning the icebreaker into an exam question. How old was Methuselah before he died? Do not put people on the spot. A great icebreaker might be, "When you were 7-12 years old, where did you live, and who were you closest to?" Thought-provoking, open-ended questions help group members to know each other more intimately.

One member in my group shared this icebreaker, "When you were young, what was your favorite sport, and share a time when things didn't go well for you when playing that Sport." .15 minutes is plenty of time for the icebreaker.

The **Worship** time is an excellent opportunity to invite the presence of Christ into the group. Many groups will use a YouTube video or playlist. With today's technology, we can invite Hillsong into the living room to lead worship. Some might have a guitarist in the group or a pianist. I just encourage groups to make sure everyone can see the words, whether that is through a screen or song-sheet. Making the lyrics available is especially important with newcomers because they do not know the songs. The worship typically lasts about 20 minutes.

I encourage groups to connect the **Word** time to the pastor's sermon. This time lasts for about .40 minutes. In other words, the pastor preaches on the passage the weekend before the small group meeting, and the group applies that same passage in the small group. Avoid saying, "the Pastor said." Instead, "The Bible says." I encourage the groups to use three simple questions based on the passage:

1. What does the Scripture passage say?
2. What is God saying to me right now through this Scripture?
3. How can I apply this Bible passage in my life during the following week?

Before answering each question, I encourage the group to read the passage and have a time of silence. After the **Word** time, I encourage groups to pray for the needs of those present.

The **Witness** time is to plan and pray for new people to come to the group. This time normally lasts about .15 minutes. Often groups will place an empty chair in the middle, praying for the next person to fill it. Maybe the group will plan a time of outreach. The goal is to pray and plan to reach a lost world for Jesus Christ.

Yes, we need to be flexible. Variety is the spice of life. However, it's also important to remember that plans are essential, and it helps to start the group with a particular order.

Reflection Questions

What did you learn from this lesson?

How will this lesson help you to change your current order?

What is the one thing you will do differently next week?

Suggested Resources

Books

- *Lesson 1 of Lead: Guide a Small Group to Experience Christ*
- *Lesson 2 of Facilitate: How to Lead a Life-Giving Small Group*
- *chapter 2 of How to Lead a Great Cell Group So People Want to Come Back*

Internet articles (available at www.joelcomiskeygroup.com/resources)

What is a Sample Cell Group Order of Meeting?
How to Prepare Great Cell Group Questions
Extra Resources to Prepare Great Cell Lessons
Cell Lessons Based on the Pastor's Sermon
The Best Cell Agenda
Aiming at Transformation in the Cell Lesson
Exciting Cell Group in Bangkok
Effective Cell Lessons
Applying God's Word

Download this PowerPoint

Joel Comiskey's PowerPoint on this lesson:

https://www.dropbox.com/s/s8ea0i70o1jdfrb/lesson2-4ws.pptx?dl=0

Edification — the essence of Small Group Ministry

WATCH THIS VIDEO ▶

https://youtu.be/i5V9hA__Y5Q

Several years ago, I visited a small group led by Myrna. She was following the regular order of the small group, but she decided to be creative during the worship time. She asked each member to pick their favorite song. Theresa, one of the members, chose a song called "Renew me." Afterward, Myrna said to Theresa, "Why did you pick that song?" Theresa began to sob, saying,

"I just found out that my husband is seeing another woman. I need renewal."

Myrna, led by the Holy Spirit, stopped everything. She asked all members to gather around Theresa to pray for her. Many prayed, and some offered words of comfort. Myrna gave Theresa the time she needed to experience God's healing touch.

Myrna's small group became a family to Theresa. I re-visited that group one year later, and Theresa was still there. Yes, her husband did leave her, but the group became a new family for her. Jesus used the loving care of the group members to minister to her deep needs during the crisis.

Sometimes we can become overly concerned about following a particular order in the small group. We want to make sure everything is "right," as if there was one right way to facilitate the small group. The reality is that the most important "right thing" to do is meet the needs of those present. And there is a biblical word that describes this truth. It is called *oikodomeo*.

The Greek word *oikodomeo* means to build up. The literal meaning is to reconstruct. Rather than following a particular order, rebuilding people's lives is at the heart of small group ministry. Jesus desires that the gospel transforms people. The noun form of *Oikodemo* is *Oikos*, which means *house* in the New Testament. Thus, *oikodomeo* means to build up or edify the house.

Extended family, which included servants, characterized the households of ancient times. The house churches primarily focused on the home, and *oikodomeo* was the focal point of those early house churches. Small groups in our day can learn a lot from those ancient house churches, and *oikodomeo* is one of those principles.

On one occasion, Frank and Kathy arrived full of fear and anxiety. They were robbed at gunpoint a few days earlier and needed comfort and a place to vent. We could have moved on to another topic, but Frank and Kathy were our focus that evening.

We listened to them, prayed for them, and read Scripture to them. They needed a spiritual family to care for their needs. Instead of following the "correct" order, we made Frank and Kathy the group's focal point. Yes, it's essential to have a plan, but more important than the order of the small group is the re-building of the members' lives.

Sometimes leaders can become discouraged when new people do not show up. But if we remember that *oikodomeo* is the goal, we can take courage to build up those present. The reality is that sometimes, the smaller number in the group can be a blessing in disguise because it allows leaders to focus on the members and their needs.

Reflection Questions

What was the main principle you learned from this lesson?

How would you describe the *oikodomeo* taking place in your group?

What do you need to do differently in your group after learning about *oikodomeo?*

Suggested Resources

Books

- *Chapter 4 of The Spirit-filled Small Group: Leading Your Group to Experience the Spiritual Gifts*
- *Lessons 5 and 7 of Facilitate: How to Lead a Life-Giving Small Group*
- *Chapters 4 and 7 of How to Lead a Great Cell Group So People Want to Come Back*

Internet articles (available at www.joelcomiskeygroup.com/resources)

How to Be A Great Cell Member
People Want to Experience God in the Cell
How God's Healing Power Can Transform the
    Cell Group
Follow the Way of Love
Confronting Problems in the Cell
Members Talking to Members
Members caring for Members
Listening Brings Healing
Balancing evangelism and edification

Download this PowerPoint

Joel Comiskey's PowerPoint on this

lesson: https://www.dr opbox.com/s/
    xwao6lgwg18sser/lesson3-edification.
    pptx?dl=0

LESSON 4

The Best Small Group Lesson

WATCH THIS VIDEO ▶

https://youtu.be/bvm8NFgIPRM

When thinking about small groups, one of the first questions is about the lesson material. What is the best lesson material to follow?

I recommend following the Scripture of the pastor's sermon. Following the same Scriptural passage connects the pastoral teaching with what takes place in the small groups. Pastors are satisfied when they know that the members will be applying the message during the week in their small groups.

I tell leaders not to mention what the pastor said but instead talk about what the Bible says. Yet, following the pastor's sermon keeps small group ministry on a solid doctrinal trajectory.

Following the pastor's sermon is a great start, but it does not clarify the questions to use. Many pastors or leaders do not know how to create dynamic questions. They might give the leader a variety of question options, but the reality is that small group leaders often do not take the time to perfect the questions. As a result, the lesson time stagnates.

I have taught a lot on this topic over the years and have tried hard in my books to explain the difference between observation, interpretation, and application questions. Yet, invariably, the leader will not make adjustments to meet the needs of their group, and the group discussion is often lifeless and close-ended.

We have been experimenting with three simple questions that have brought new life to our groups and many other groups in the last several years. These three questions are straightforward:

1. What does the passage say?
2. What is Holy Spirit saying to you through this passage?

3. How can you apply these verses to your life during the next week?

With the question "what is the passage saying?" the leader is trying to find out what the text says. Members often want to rush into an application question. But we need to hold off and just find out what God is saying in his Word. Only as we understand the actual context will we be able to apply it accurately. God has inspired the Bible and made it clear and understandable. We need first to discover the real meaning.

The second question is, "What is God saying to me through this passage?" This question is more personal and should inspire transparency. Notice the question is not saying, "What is God saying to other people?" Some people in the group like to answer this question by talking about what others should do. But the question asks each member to share what God is speaking to them about in their own lives. The goal of this question is transformation rather than more information—or worse yet, talking about what other people should do.

Then the third question is, "What can I do in the following week to apply this passage of Scripture?" The goal of the third question is to determine how each member can practically apply this passage.

Now let's describe this process in more detail.

I encourage leaders to ask someone in the group to read the passage. It is always good to get as many people participating as possible. However, do not ask someone who is new or might be hesitant to read.

Then ask the first question. What is this passage saying? Before people answer, ask everyone to take a moment of silence. Pausing before answering the question gives everyone a chance to think about the Bible verses before answering.

After people have answered the first question, reread the passage and ask, "What is the Holy Spirit saying to you through these verses?" But before responding, ask the group to take a moment of silence. They must be meditating on the Scripture before responding.

Be sure to include as many people as possible in the discussion. I like it when the leader says, "Let's start with those who didn't answer the first question."

After answering the second question, ask someone else to reread the passage. After hearing the Bible verses for the third time, ask the question, "how are you going to apply this passage during the upcoming week?" Before talking about it, take another time of silence.

With these three questions, we have experienced vibrant discussion. We've also witnessed people leading the lesson time who never felt capable beforehand. This method is simple and helps everyone to focus on transformation rather than information.

Reflection Questions

What is the main principle that you've learned from this lesson?

What lesson material have you previously been using?

How will these three questions change what you are currently doing in your group?

Suggested Resources

Books

- *Chapter 5 of How to Lead a Great Cell Group So People Want to Come Back*
- *Lesson 5 of Facilitate: How to Lead a Life-Giving Small Group*
- *Lesson 2 of Lead: Guide a Small Group to Experience Christ*

Internet articles (available at www.joelcomiskeygroup.com/resources)

How to Prepare Great Cell Group Questions
Extra Resources to Prepare Great Cell Lessons
Cell Lessons Based on the Pastor's Sermon
The Best Cell Agenda
Aiming at Transformation in the Cell Lesson
Ministering to One Another in the Cell
Exciting Cell Group in Bangkok
Effective Cell Lessons
Applying God's Word
Cell Lesson: Spener and Pietism
Cell Lesson: Key tips
Cell Lesson: Preparing Yourself
Cell Lesson: Preparing the Lesson
Cell Lesson: Introducing the Lesson
Cell Lesson: Flexible Planning
Cell Lesson: Allowing the Spirit to Move

Download this PowerPoint

Joel Comiskey's PowerPoint on this lesson:

*https://www.dropbox.com/s/tlw1hlpep5ja4zj/
lesson4-questions.pptx?dl=0*

LESSON 5

Characteristics of effective small group leadership — Filling of the Spirit, Facilitation, and Listening

WATCH THIS VIDEO ▶

https://youtu.be/DdKIT24iscg

The character of the leader is more important than leadership skills. People will ultimately follow the leader's example, so the leader must be Spirit-controlled. Along with a Spirit-led life are other critical characteristics, like facilitation and listening.

Filling of the Holy Spirit

Small group leaders simply don't know all that is going to happen in the meeting. Maybe a baby will start crying, a dog might bark, or the leader might forget the questions. Yet, the leader filled with the Holy Spirit will have the insight to know what to do next. The Spirit will bring back to their memory his wisdom.

Jesus said that he would send the Holy Spirit to guide believers into all truth and show them what to do next (John 16:7-8). The Holy Spirit dwells within each believer, and he wants to control and guide them.

I tell small group leaders to stop preparing for the group lesson, the refreshments, or the arrangement of chairs. Instead, spend time with the Holy Spirit, who will guide the leader into all truth. I urge leaders to spend at least .15 minutes and maybe .30 minutes just waiting on the Lord before the group starts, asking God to fill them. He will (Luke 11:13).

Facilitate

The word "leader" often has negative implications. Some imagine images of control or domination. On the other hand, the word facilitate *means* empowering, making it easy, or helping someone.

And remember, the group's goal is to make disciples who make disciples (Matthew 28:18-20). Discipleship takes place when we allow people to make mistakes and fail forward. People learn through trial and error. They do not mature and grow by sitting and listening. Instead, they learn through active participation.

For facilitation to happen, it's essential to arrange the chairs in a circle so the members can talk to one another. No one should be hiding behind someone else, as if they were listening to the speaker. Instead, they should be looking and ministering to each other. Everyone should be face to face which helps in the facilitation of the group.

Listening

The best facilitators listen intently to everyone in the group, teaching the members to do the same. James says, "My dear brothers and sisters, take note of this: Everyone should be quick to listen, slow to speak and slow to become angry" (James 1:19).

And listening is not only to the words but also gestures and non-verbal cues. Experts say that some

70% to 90% of communication is non-verbal. Effective small group facilitators recognize through non-verbal communication when a person wants to interject a comment or when others register confusion.

The leader is also communicating non-verbally by their reactions. I tell leaders to admit if they are tired from a difficult day of work. Let the members know before the group so that if the leader yawns, it is not because of the member's response.

The leader should teach the members to listen intently. I have noticed that often the members are only concerned about what they are going to say rather than proactively listening to what others are saying. The best groups practice proactive listening among the members.

Reflection Questions

What is the central truth that you've learned from this lesson?

Of the three characteristics mentioned in this lesson, what do you need to work on most?

How can you apply these characteristics?

How can your group apply these characteristics in the small group?

Suggested Resources

Books

- chapters 1,2 & 4 of *The Spirit-filled Small Group: Leading Your Group to Experience the Spiritual Gifts*
- lesson 1 of *Discover: Use Your Gifts and Help Others Find Theirs*
- chapter 3 & 6 of *How to Lead a Great Cell Group Meeting: So People Want to Come Back*

Internet articles (available at www.joelcomiskeygroup.com/resources)

Daily Soul Care for Cell Leaders
Spending Time with Jesus
Starting the Year Right with Jesus
Hindrances to Spending Time with Jesus
The Filling of the Holy Spirit: What It Is
The Filling of the Holy Spirit: How to Receive It
Stop Talking
Listening Brings Healing
How to Practice Effective Listening
You Can Be a Better Listener

Download this PowerPoint

Joel Comiskey's PowerPoint on this lesson:

*https://www.dropbox.com/s/
    m86x6770nvq01nw/lesson5-
    fillingSpiritFacilitateListening.pptx?dl=0*

Characteristics of effective small group leadership — Transparency, Encouragement, and Dealing with the Talker

WATCH THIS VIDEO ▶

https://youtu.be/-ME_isDTijE

The best small group leaders possess specific characteristics that make them fruitful in facilitating small groups. They are willing to share transparently rather than boasting of their accomplishments. They encourage those who share rather than expecting only one answer. They are also ready to deal with conflict, like those who talk too much in the group.

Transparency

Some leaders see themselves as Bible teachers who are supposed to provide Bible knowledge to hungry hearers. Dynamic small groups, however, avoid the lecture mentality and promote participation that leads to transformation. James writes, "Therefore confess your sins to each other and pray for each other so that you may be healed. The prayer of a righteous person is powerful and effective" (James 5:16).

Transparency needs to start with the leader. If the leader tries to impress or act super spiritual, the members will also resist sharing freely. I have been present in groups where members tried to share deep struggles and hurt but didn't receive encouragement from the leader. These members felt like they needed to give the correct answers and appear spiritual. When members share struggles, they need leaders to listen and acknowledge the pain.

For many years, I've led or attended a small group. I believe in small group ministry and need community. I've always attempted to share honestly in the group about my struggles and needs. My transparency encourages others to share freely as well. We also must remember that transparent sharing is not limited to talking about difficult experiences. It also includes revealing victories and the positive things that God is doing.

Encouragement

When members share transparently, it takes courage. They need positive feedback to continue. The answers to the small group questions do not require just one correct answer. Unlike exam questions, small group sharing applies God's Word to human needs. And because each person is at a different place in life, no one answer will meet each person's needs.

I visited one group in which the leader acted like there was just one right and wrong answer. When someone would share, he would say, "not quite right, but you're getting closer." Someone else would share, and he would also give them a similar answer, "warmer but not there yet." I remember that by the end of the small group lesson, no one wanted to share. Silence. The members did not want to risk being hurt by the leader.

The small group focuses on making disciples who make disciples. To do that effectively, each member needs the freedom to share what is really going on inside.

Dealing with the Talker

If the small group is about making disciples through participation, one person should not dominate the meeting. Being a great facilitator means empowering everyone to talk and share, not just one or two people. So, what is the best way to deal with those who talk too much?

One easy way to deal with the talker is to start the question with, "Let's start with those who have not responded yet."

My favorite way is to call on people by name. "What do you think, Mary?" "how about you, John?" But do not call on the person who already talks too much.

It might be a good idea to sit by the talker to avoid giving them eye contact.

A more radical way is when the talker pauses to say, "what do the rest of you think?" The problem with this approach is that often the talker does not pause!

One of the best ways is to use the Jesus strategy and go directly to the talker (Matthew 18). Just tell the person that the purpose of the group is to get everyone to talk. You might even ask them to help you get others to speak. Maybe they will get the hint that they have been talking too much.

Reflection Questions

What is the primary truth that you have learned from this lesson?

Of the three characteristics mentioned in this lesson, what do you need to work on most?

How can you as a leader apply these characteristics?

How can your group apply these characteristics?

Suggested Resources

Books

- *Chapters 4,7 of How to Lead a Great Cell Group Meeting: So People Want to Come Back*
- *Chapter 4 of The Spirit-filled Small Group: Leading Your Group to Experience the Spiritual Gifts*

Internet articles (available at www.joelcomiskeygroup.com/resources)

Transparency: Don't Hide Behind Curriculum
Transparency in the Cell Group
Transparency Killers
Transparency: Lead the Way
Aiming at Transformation in the Cell Lesson
How God's Healing Power Can Transform the Cell Group
The Power of Encouragement
Loving Others—Even When You Don't Feel Like It
Follow the Way of Love
Confronting Problems in the Cell
How to be a Great Cell Member
Members Talking to Members
Members caring for Members
Dealing with the Talkers
Common Group Problems

Download this PowerPoint

Joel Comiskey's PowerPoint on this lesson:

https://www.dropbox.com/s/o02e5fra0lre78s/ lesson6-transparencyEncouragementTalker. pptx?dl=0

Gifts of the Spirit and Small Group Ministry — Definition and Usage

WATCH THIS VIDEO ▶

https://youtu.be/w4nZHRNnPck

I remember talking to a pastor who said, "Joel, you should explore the relationship between small groups and the gifts of the Spirit. Most of the literature on the gifts of the Spirit centers on ministries and programs rather than small groups." His words confirmed the need to write a book on the topic. I already knew that the New Testament writers wrote the gift passages to those attending house churches, but this pastor's words gave me new urgency to pursue this topic.

When Paul wrote about the gifts of the Spirit in 1 Corinthians 12-14, Romans 12, and Ephesians 4, he envisioned a small group of people who were practicing the gifts of the Spirit. Paul's letters were passed around from house to house. Peter also talks about the gifts of the Spirit in chapter 4 of his first letter.

All the gift passages assumed the context of the early house church. The New Testament house church environment was the perfect place to discover a person's gift and use those gifts. In this loving, caring atmosphere, people were encouraged to use their God-given gift (s).

The word *gift* is the Greek word *Charisma* and comes from the Greek word *Charis,* or grace. God's gifts are his graces given to the church. John Wimber used the term *graceletts* to describe the gifts because God gives them freely and sovereignly. The New Testament defines twenty-one gifts, but some authors add gifts from the Old Testament and write about twenty-seven or twenty-eight gifts.

Only believers have gifts. When a person is born again, they receive at least one gift, but often more.

Peter writes, "Each of you should use whatever gift you have received to serve others, as faithful stewards of God's grace in its various forms" (1 Peter 4:10).

I believe the gifts are permanent because Paul uses body parts to describe the gifts of the Spirit in 1 Corinthians 12 and Romans 12. However, God can give new gifts to anyone or even a group of people according to present needs. He is sovereign and pours out his Spirit and gifts as he sees fit.

Natural talents are different than spiritual gifts. Christians and non-Christians possess natural skills that develop over time. Someone might be talented in fixing cars, making furniture, or sewing quilts. A person might be a competent high school teacher without the gift of teaching. Bruce Bugbee, an expert on the gifts of the Spirit, administered a study of 10,000 Christians to discover a connection between spiritual giftedness and natural talents. He concluded that there was no connection.

Christian responsibilities are also distinct from spiritual gifts. All believers should evangelize, but certain ones have the gift of evangelism. All believers should serve others, but certain believers have the gift of service. All believers should tithe and give offerings, but certain ones have the gift of giving.

Some pastors have not wanted to talk about spiritual gifts because some people use their giftedness as an excuse for not fulfilling their Christian responsibilities. "I don't want to help John move to a new house because I don't have the gift of helps," they might say. Or "I'm not going to evangelize with the group because I don't have the gift of evangelism." God's inerrant Word must guide all we do and say regardless of a believer's particular giftedness.

Many small group leaders feel weighed down because they are not allowing gifted members to help carry the burden. They are trying to do everything themselves instead of calling on members to serve and use their gifts. When the leader realizes that everyone has at least one spiritual gift, the weight of trying to do everything fades away.

God knew what he was doing when he gave birth to the early church in small groups. He wanted each member to understand their role in the body of Christ. God's plan is the same in the church today. Small groups are the best atmosphere to make mistakes, get feedback, and discover God-given spiritual gifts.

Reflection Questions

What is the central truth that you have learned from
this lesson?

How can you apply the teaching on spiritual gifts to
your small group?

How will you encourage the members to use their
gifts?

Suggested Resources

Books

– *Lessons 2, 3, 7,8 of Discover: Use Your Gifts
and Help Others Find Theirs*
– *Chapters 5, 6 of The Spirit-filled Small
Group: Leading Your Group to Experience the
Spiritual Gifts*

Internet articles (available at
www.joelcomiskeygroup.com/resources)

Scriptural Basis for Gift Use in Cells
Why Cells Effectively Develop the Spiritual Gifts
Cells and the Gifts of the Spirit
Using the Gifts of the Spirit in the Cell Church

Growth through Using the Spiritual Gifts
Dangers of Gift Use in the Cell Church
Motivating Others to Use Their Spiritual Gifts

Download this PowerPoint

Joel Comiskey's PowerPoint on this lesson:

https://www.dropbox.com/s/k8pcdk2v1ebageq/
lesson7-spiritualGiftsBiblicalUse.
pptx?dl=0

LESSON 8

Gifts of the Spirit and Small Group Ministry — Variety and Identification

WATCH THIS VIDEO ▶

https://youtu.be/axJRUHqbrvc

The best small group leaders are the ones filled with the Holy Spirit. They have spent time with Jesus and lead the group under Christ's direction. Like the leader, the best small groups prioritize the Spirit's presence. The Holy Spirit permeates the group and directs the members to use their gifts.

The New Testament context for spiritual gift use is the small group. Each biblical gift passage has the house church context in mind since house churches met throughout the Roman empire during the first century. And every born-again believer has at least one spiritual gift. The apostle Peter says, "Each of you should use whatever gift you have received to serve others, as faithful stewards of God's grace in its various forms" (1 Peter 4:10).

So how do we know what gift (s) we possess? The first step is to understand what the New Testament says about the gifts of the Spirit. I have counted twenty-one gifts in the New Testament, although some authors on spiritual gifts talk about twenty-seven or twenty-eight. Those who see additional gifts are counting possible gifts from the Old Testament. Apart from those Old Testament gifts, here is what I see in the New Testament:

The service gifts

- Helps (1 Corinthians 12:28)
- Service (Romans 12:7)
- Giving (Romans 12:8)
- Administration (1 Corinthians 12:28)
- Mercy (Romans 12:8)
- Faith (1 Corinthians 12:9)

I believe that God has given the church an abundance of *help* and *service* gifts. Christian Schwarz, a respected Christian author on the gifts of the Spirit, believes this as well. Knowing this truth can alleviate burdened small group leaders to share the load with others. Remember, those with the gifts of helps and service want to serve others. If you do not give them something to do, they will feel unwanted.

The *equipping gifts* describe another category of gifts.

Equipping Gifts

- Exhortation (Romans 12:8)
- Wisdom (1 Corinthians 12:8)
- Knowledge (1 Corinthians 12:8)
- Teaching (1 Corinthians 12:28)
- Pastoring (Ephesians 4:11)
- Leadership (Romans 12:8)
- Apostleship (1 Corinthians 12:28)
- Evangelism (Ephesians 4:11)

The equipping gifts strengthen God's people to grow in maturity. Paul tells us that God has called apostles, teachers, and other leaders "to equip his people for works of service, so that the body of Christ may be built up until we all reach unity in the faith and in the knowledge of the Son of God and become mature, attaining to the whole measure of the fullness of Christ" (Ephesians 4:12-13). Finally, Scripture gives us the prayer and worship gifts.

Prayer and Worship gifts

- Prophecy (1 Corinthians 12:10)
- Tongues (1 Corinthians 12:10)
- Interpretation of tongues (1 Corinthians 12:10)
- Healing (1 Corinthians 12:9)
- Miracles (1 Corinthians 12:10)
- Discernment of spirits (1 Corinthians 12:10)

Many refer to these gifts as supernatural gifts. The gift of tongues gets a lot of publicity, but it's just one gift among many. The gift of tongues is a wonderful gift to use in a person's prayer time as a personal prayer language. But when using this gift publicly, it should always be accompanied by the interpretation of tongues.

The Bible tells us that the church should exercise the gifts in an orderly way because God is a God of order. Paul says, "For God is not a God of disorder but of peace—as in all the congregations of the Lord's people" (1 Corinthians 14: 33).

Some pastors don't promote spiritual gifts because they are afraid of wildfire (the misuse of the gifts). Small group leaders should learn how to lead the gift use in the small group so that peace and order reign. At the same time, I've noticed that many small groups are dry with little expectancy because they don't allow the Holy Spirit to operate through the giftedness of each member.

I go into more detail about the gifts and gift usage in my book *Discover* and *The Spirit-filled Small Group*.

Beyond understanding the number and definition of New Testament gifts is learning God's gifting to each believer. We know that each believer has at least one gift (1 Peter 4:8). But how do we know what gift (s) God has given to each believer?

The first place to look is desire. What does a person like to do? Do they enjoy clarifying passages of Scripture? Maybe they have the gift of teaching. Do they want to help other people when they have a need? Perhaps they have the gift of helps or service. Do they delight in receiving a Word from the Lord? Maybe they have the gift of prophecy.

Another way to know a gift is through confirmation. Those in the small group confirm the giftedness of each member. The small group is intimate enough to allow each person to step out with confidence and exercise spiritual gifts. Because groups are small, it is okay to fail and experiment with various gifts. When someone has a particular gift, they should expect fruit. For example, if someone has the gift of teaching, people will understand Scripture better. If they have the gift of evangelism, non-Christians will become believers.

Spiritual gifts help small groups become more dynamic as members watch with expectancy for what God will do in their midst.

Reflection Questions

What is the main truth that you learned from this lesson?

How can you apply the truths in this lesson to your small group?

What will you do to discern and use your particular spiritual gift?

Suggested Resources

Books

- Lessons 4-6 of Discover: Discover: Use Your Gifts and Help Others Find Theirs
- Chapter 7-9 of The Spirit-filled Small Group: Leading Your Group to Experience the Spiritual Gifts

Internet articles (available at www.joelcomiskeygroup.com/resources)

How the Gifts Work in the Small Group Ministering to One Another through the Gift of Prophecy

Download this PowerPoint

Joel Comiskey's PowerPoint on this lesson:

https://www.dropbox.com/s/azc6vazrqbftk9k/ lesson8-spiritualGiftsVarietyApplication. pptx?dl=0

Evangelism — Why Group Outreach is Essential

WATCH THIS VIDEO ▶

https://youtu.be/DVZReBTeNfg

We have a wonderful gospel. Jesus Christ, God incarnate, came down to this earth, lived a perfect life, died for our sins, and rose again. The Bible tells us that whoever believes in Jesus has eternal life. What great news!

Now that great news is placed upon a very dark backdrop, which is the reality of sin. All humanity is born in sin. We are sinners by nature. No amount of good works can be sufficient to make us right before God. God will only accept us if we place our faith in Jesus Christ, who took our sins on himself. When we trust Jesus, we become right and pure before God. We need to share this good news at every opportunity.

Often when talking about evangelism, we think of one-on-one evangelism. The most common type of evangelism in the New Testament, however, is group evangelism.

The New Testament church was group-oriented and part of a collective culture. When Jesus tells his disciples that he would make them fishers of men, he was not thinking about fishing with a pole to catch one fish at a time.

Rather, he was thinking about net fishing. The disciples threw out their nets together and worked as a team because they were net fishermen. They would reel in those nets together with the hope of catching a lot of fish. And group evangelism is all about team unity and outreach.

The group prays, plans, and then evangelizes together. Yes, each person has a particular role, but the team makes the catch.

When Jesus gave his disciples the great commission in Matthew 28: 18-20, he had a group in mind. Jesus had already sent them out two-by-two into the homes (Matthew 10; Luke 9,10), and now he was asking them to form new groups of disciples. The implication was that they would meet in the houses to make those disciples.

In my book *Making Disciples in the 21st Century Church,* I have a chapter on making disciples through evangelistic outreach. As each group member reaches out, they become like Jesus in the process. We must resist the mentality that the group is only about fellowship or community. Evangelism is essential.

Some churches think that if the group reaches out and new people are coming, the group will have less intimacy. And because of this fear, many groups do not evangelize. However, Jim Egli and I discovered this was not true, and we recorded our findings in our book *Groups that Thrive.* We based our research on a questionnaire that 1800 leaders in four languages completed.

We found that the group grew in deeper intimacy as it reached non-Christians with the gospel. On the other hand, closed, non-evangelizing groups were less intimate with each other. Surprisingly, evangelism draws the group closer together in the process of reaching out.

We have great news to share because Jesus is the way, the truth, and the life. No one can come to the Father except through him. Small group ministry is deeply rooted in biblical history. Jesus chose the small group strategy to grow his disciples and reach people in the process. We must do the same.

Reflection Questions

What is the principal truth that you have learned from this lesson?

How does small group evangelism help the group to become more like Jesus?

What is your group doing to reach out?

What is the next step in small group outreach in your group?

Suggested resources

Books

- *Lessons 1,2,5,6 of Share: Make Christ Real to Others*
- *Chapter 1,2,8 of Home Cell Group Explosion: How Your Small Group Can Grow and Multiply*
- *Chapter 8 of How to Lead a Great Cell Group Meeting: So People Want to Come Back*

Internet articles (available at www.joelcomiskeygroup.com/resources)

Discipleship through Group Evangelism
Holiness Evangelism
Truth and Myth about Evangelism and Community
Outreach through Small Groups
Positioning Cells to Evangelize
Taking the Church to the People
Missions and Cell Ministry
Go and Preach the Gospel to All Peoples
Catching a Passion for Cell Evangelism
Cells and Missions
Missions: What Is It?
Missions: The Reasons We Are Still on Earth
Evangelistic Cell Lessons
Myth: The Cell Church Doesn't Work
Looking Back at Home Cell Group Explosion
Power of Prayer in Cell Evangelism
Group Evangelism: Reach Out to Grow Closer
Group Evangelism: Community and Evangelism
    Go Together
Group Evangelism: Praying Together for the Lost
Group Evangelism: Don't Neglect the Witness
    Time
Group Evangelism: Facilitating Group Outreach
Jesus Changes Everything
Inviting Those Who Do Not Regularly Attend the
    Cell Group
Don't Neglect to Exercise Your Evangelistic
    Muscles
Reaching People During Covid-19

Download this PowerPoint

Joel Comiskey's PowerPoint on this lesson:

*https://www.dropbox.com/
s/9l8aae22bt0ixdy/lesson9-
smallGroupEvangelismBiblicalBase.
pptx?dl=0*

Evangelism — Strategies for Group Evangelism

WATCH THIS VIDEO ▶

https://youtu.be/h-EW7N34R6I

The gospel is the good news that Jesus Christ, the Son of God, came to this earth, lived a perfect life, and then died on the cross for the world's sins. Scripture says that whoever believes in him will have eternal life (John 3:16). We have amazing news to share in our small groups. But how can groups most effectively reach out?

The first and foremost strategy is prayer. Prayer is not just a strategy or technique—it's the oxygen of the church. We need to start with prayer because the reality is that only God can convert a lost soul. Scripture tells us that the god of this age has blinded the minds of those who do not believe (2 Corinthians 4:4). Satan has deceived non-Christians, so they cannot see the light of the glorious gospel of Jesus.

One prayer strategy that many small groups use is called the *Blessing List*. The leader asks each member to offer two names of close contacts to whom they are evangelizing. I'm referring to friends, relatives, or work associates—those the member regularly contacts. The leader gathers those names and places them on a general list. The small group prays each week for that list. The members "bless" those on the list and pray for open doors to reach out to them.

Another excellent prayer strategy is the *empty chair*. The leader or member places an empty chair in the middle of the group, and the group prays for the next person to fill it. You might have each member picture someone in their mind who they would like to see sitting in the chair. Then one or two people pray for God to fill the empty chair.

While prayer touches on the unseen, spiritual backdrop of outreach, *meeting the needs of non-Christians*, is a time-tested strategy to prepare people to hear the good news of the gospel. David Cho, the pastor of the largest church in the history of Christianity, has perfected this strategy. He tells his group leaders not to share the gospel immediately. Instead, he tells them first to meet people's needs, build a relationship with them, and then share the gospel. Meeting needs will not save anyone. Only believing the gospel message converts people. Satisfying felt needs, however, is a great way to soften hearts and prepare the soil for the gospel.

While preparing to write the book *Passion and Persistence* about the Elim Church in El Salvador, I interviewed Josephina. She was a Jehovah's Witness who resisted the gospel message. But she also lived next door to an Elim cell group, which met every Saturday night. She would hear them worshiping, but she had no desire to join the group since she was a Jehovah's Witness. Yet, the members reached out to her in practical ways. They asked her if they could voluntarily babysit her children, so she could continue working. Her husband was abusive, so she welcomed all the help she could find.

Slowly God melted her heart. She eventually attended an Elim cell group, received Jesus, and never looked back. When I talked to her, she had already opened her own home to host several small groups.

In my book, *Share: Make Christ Real to Others,* I talk about various group strategies. For example, many small groups have barbeques or picnics, inviting those who do not know Jesus. Others plan to go to an event together, like a sports activity, so they can invite non-Christians to go with them. Others might set up a table at a large store or public gatherings to give out free water on a hot day, pray for people, or give out gospel tracts.

Many groups rotate the meeting place because non-Christians are more receptive to enter a home they have already visited. When the small group is in a family member's house, the non-Christian is far more likely to participate in the group meeting. Rotation is a great way to open new outreach opportunities.

As the small group prays and strategizes together, God will open new doors to share the gospel of Jesus Christ. We have a wonderful gospel, and God wants us to creatively think about ways to share it. The key is prayerfully planning as a group to reach out and moving forward with those plans.

Reflection Questions

What is the key truth that you have learned from
this lesson?

How has your group evangelized in the past?

From reading this lesson, what evangelistic strategy
would work best for your group?

List two non-Christians friends who you are praying
for currently.

Suggested resources

Books

- *Lessons 3,4,7,8 of Share: Make Christ Real to Others*
- *Chapter 4,7, 9 of Home Cell Group Explosion: How Your Small Group Can Grow and Multiply*
- *Chapter 8 of How to Lead a Great Cell Group Meeting: So People Want to Come Back*

Internet articles (available at www.joelcomiskeygroup.com/resources)

Six Keys to Evangelistic Success in Cell Ministry
Using the Empty Chair to Reach Out
Social Outreach through Cell Ministry

Friendship Evangelism in the Cell Church
Effective Cell Evangelism
Reaching People Unlike Us
Reaching ethnic groups through cells
Homogenous Cell Evangelism (Dr. Mike Erickson)
Recovery Cell Outreach
Reaching New Neighbors for Jesus (Michael Sove)
Church Growth Rates Depend on the Soil
Spending Time with Unbelievers
Redemption and Lift
Baptismal Testimony
Strategies of Prayer in Cell Evangelism
Don't Limit the Evangelism Method

Download this PowerPoint

Joel Comiskey's PowerPoint on this lesson:

https://www.dropbox.com/s/ w1aw714e4wnibac/lesson10- smallGroupEvangelismStrategies. pptx?dl=0

Multiplication — Making Disciples Who Make Disciples

WATCH THIS VIDEO ▶

https://youtu.be/rs4AzMh26HM

W hen I first started studying small group ministry, I thought that the group's main goal was to have a great time of fellowship.

But then I started studying small group-based churches worldwide and noticed that their small groups evangelized and multiplied. I realized that multiplication was an essential factor in dynamic small groups and small group-based churches.

I wrote the book *Home Cell Group Explosion* and *Leadership Explosion* to describe what I witnessed.

Yet, I also noticed a danger. It was possible to multiply too rapidly and lose the quality. Some churches and leaders were so focused on the goal of multiplication that the group gave birth before it was truly ready. Sometimes the pressure to reproduce drove leaders to multiply weak cells.

Admittedly, I have done this on various occasions. I was overly interested in fulfilling the goal of multiplication to the detriment of producing quality disciples to lead the new groups.

I now believe that making disciples needs to be the primary motivation of small group ministry, including multiplication. Making disciples is the primary focus in my definition of a small group:

Groups of 3-15 people who meet weekly outside the church building for the purpose of evangelism, community, and spiritual growth with the goal of making disciples who make disciples that results in multiplication.

Notice the goal of this definition is to make disciples who make disciples. The goal is not to multiply the group. I heard one famous cell church pastor say, "Healthy cells multiply." So what makes a healthy small group? Those groups that are producing disciples. But how does this happen?

In my book *Making Disciples in the 21st Century Church*, I describe how cell-based churches make disciples, both from the standpoint of the small group and the small group system.

On the group level, disciples develop through:

- Community
- Participation
- Evangelism
- Multiplication

On the small group system level, disciples mature through:

- Celebration
- Equipping
- Coaching

Let us take a closer look at how disciples grow through the small group:

Community plays a critical role in developing disciples. Disciples mature as they learn to serve each other and overcome conflict. Unless the mother group has learned to love one another, the daughter group will be dysfunctional and manifest the same problems.

Participation emphasizes the priesthood of all believers. Each member needs to exercise their spiritual gifts and participate in each group function: icebreaker, worship, lesson, and witness time. In my group, for example, we rotate among the leadership team, even with the lesson time. The small group lesson needs to be simple enough for each person on the leadership team to take a turn (see lesson 4). If members do not exercise their muscles by participating in the mother group, they will be unprepared to lead the daughter cell. If the members are not practicing their spiritual gifts in the mother group, they will not know how to practice them in the daughter group.

Evangelism. Jesus is the only way to have a relationship with the Father and enter heaven. And those who reject Jesus are choosing to go to hell. We should have an urgency to share the gospel. But another crucial motivation to evangelize is to exercise spiritual muscles in the process of becoming a disciple of Jesus. Group members become like Jesus as they pray for their non-Christian friends, find a need and meet it, and invite their friends and neighbors to the group. Reaching out to unbelievers helps the cell members become disciples of Christ because they cry out to Jesus for strength to share the gospel, and in the process, become like him.

Cell system: the celebration service (preaching and worship), the equipping track, and the coaching make up the cell system. Sunday celebration is an essential part of the discipleship system. Members come together to hear God's Word, worship together, and receive God's vision. They become like Jesus in the process. Equipping is another vital aspect of discipleship. Everyone in the church is encouraged to complete the equipping. They are ready to participate as part of the leadership team in a new cell group when they graduate. Coaching is also essential. After becoming a leader, everyone in the small group-based church receives coaching from someone else. In this way, they receive ministry as they also minister to others.

Multiplication is the result of becoming Christ's disciple. Jesus desires new healthy cell groups, which translates into more and better disciples. As group members exercise their spiritual muscles and develop new disciples, Christ's church will flourish and multiply.

Reflection Questions

What is the primary truth that you have learned from this lesson?

How has your understanding changed about the goal of the small group?

What can your small group improve in the process of making disciples who make disciples?

Suggested resources

Books

- *Chapters 2,3,4,5,6,7,8,9 of Making Disciples in the 21st Century Church:*

Internet articles (available at www.joelcomiskeygroup.com/resources)

Discipleship through Multiplication
Multiplication is the Result of Making Disciples
Multiplication: Count the Cost
Two Extremes in Cell Multiplication
The Strength of Smaller Cell Groups
When it Hurts to Multiply
Keeping the Motivation Pure
Cell Ministry is All About Sending
Finding and Running with the Excited Ones

The Role of the Associate in Cell Multiplication
Why Multiplication is Necessary
How Frequently Should Cells Multiply?
Different Ways to Multiply Cell Groups

Download this PowerPoint

Joel Comiskey's PowerPoint on this lesson:

https://www.dropbox.com/s/tezjuyx0y0b5uma/
lesson11-makingDisciplesMultiplication.
pptx?dl=0

Myths and Truths about Multiplication

WATCH THIS VIDEO ▶

https://youtu.be/3e7HaFvOMiY

The topic of small group multiplication is both exciting and full of controversy. Some churches resist small group ministry because of what they have heard about multiplication—like all groups must multiply after six months or close. In my book *Myths and Truths of Cell-based Ministry*, I talk about the myths and truths of multiplication. So what are some of those myths? Here are a few:

All cells must multiply in six months or be closed. Closing groups that didn't multiply was a common myth in the early days of the cell church movement. I remember visiting a famous cell church led by Werner Kniesel in Zurich, Switzerland. He told me that various small group gurus had come to his church proclaiming that all groups needed to multiply within six months. Werner said, "It takes at least two years to multiply a small group here in Zurich." Yet, Werner patiently guided his church to transition and multiply cells, becoming a model cell church in Europe.

My good friend Raymond Ebbett was both a missionary in Bogota, Colombia, and Spain. The small groups in Bogota often multiplied in six months, but those in Spain took many years. The difference? The soil. The soil in Bogota was ready to produce the crop, but Spain's ground was hard and dry with little immediate potential. Raymond understood that the preparation of the soil was a critical component in small group multiplication.

Small group multiplication means people are being saved, maturing as disciples, and taking the church-wide equipping to become future leaders. If no one comes to Christ, very few will be equipped and ready to multiply. The opposite is true in receptive countries to the gospel. We need to have discernment, patience and avoid dogmatism that says all groups must multiply in six months. The reality is that multiplication time frames vary depending on the state of the soil.

There is only one way to multiply a cell. In the early days of the cell church movement, the most common way to reproduce a group was mother-daughter multiplication. When a group grew to a certain number, half of the group—along with a new leadership team--would leave to start the daughter group. The problem with this type of multiplication was that when a group reached a specific number, like fifteen, many people would stop coming because they did not want to "divide."

However, another great way to multiply a group is *cell planting*. As soon as a team takes the church-wide equipping and graduates, that team can leave the mother cell and start a new one, regardless of the size of the mother group.

One effective way to practice *cell planting* is for the group leader to take one or two members and plant a new group. The leader should leave the most mature behind when starting the new group.

While mother-daughter multiplication is still a great way to multiply groups, it is not the only way.

One leader should lead more than one group. I find this error is common in churches that are trying hard to reach their goals. To reach the determined year-end multiplication goal, some leaders lead more than one group. The problem with this is that the biblical goal is not more groups but more leaders or disciples. The small group strategy is about developing an army of disciples who make disciples, not new groups. It is best to have a team of leaders per group and not multiply until leaders are ready to lead the new group.

Evangelism is the same as multiplication. I hear this a lot when talking about multiplication. Sometimes people equate evangelism with multiplication, yet multiplication is much more than evangelism. To multiply a group, a leader must do many things well: evangelism, small group dynamics, conflict resolution, community, and total participation of members. Evangelism is simply one aspect of group life. Therefore, when a leader has multiplied the group, this person should be honored because it means they have done many things well.

The more we can understand the myths and pitfalls of multiplication, the more we will avoid those dangers. Yes, multiplication is essential, but small group ministry involves more than multiplication.

Reflection Questions

What is the main truth that you have learned from this lesson?

What is one of the pitfalls that you've faced in your small group ministry?

Knowing there are various ways to multiply a small group, what path have you found most effective?

Suggested resources

Books

– read chapters 3,5,6,7,8, 9 of *Myths and Truths of Cell-based Ministry: Key Principles that Make or Break Cell Ministry*

Internet articles (available at www.joelcomiskeygroup.com/resources)

Multiplication: helps and hindrances
Don't Force Multiplication
Avoiding Cell Church Legalism

Download this PowerPoint

Joel Comiskey's PowerPoint on this lesson:

*https://www.dropbox.com/s/9wc2fh4ztip6tgs/
lesson12-mythsTruthsMultiplication.
pptx?dl=0*

LESSON 13

Anyone Can Lead a Small Group

WATCH THIS VIDEO ▶

https://youtu.be/u8s2yYgbukl

When I do small group seminars around the world, I often start with the question, "What are the reasons that you have used or heard others use for not being able to lead a small group?" I get varied responses, and here are just a few:

- I'm not prepared.
- I don't have the right gifts.

- I don't have enough education.
- I don't have enough time.

The answers are so distinct that I have never cataloged all of them.

I have always been curious about what makes an effective small group leader who can multiply their small group. And this curiosity drove me to prepare a 29-question survey as part of my Ph.D. in Intercultural Studies at Fuller Seminary. I received help from others to develop the study and additional support in analyzing it. We asked 700 small group leaders in eight countries to fill out the questionnaire. The survey data helped us to determine critical factors behind small group multiplication.

Question 27 said, "Have you multiplied your group?" Question 28 said, "When was the last time you multiplied your group?" Question 29 said, "How many times have you multiplied your small group?"

The other 26 questions were independent variables with questions about giftedness, education, personality, and so forth. We then compared the 26-questions with the multiplication questions (#27-29). The findings were informative and embodied in my first book *Home Cell Group Explosion*. Here are a few insights from the study:

Personality

In designing the questionnaire, we got help from an expert in psychology and statistics to make sure we could draw out a person's true personality. The survey showed that personality was not a factor in small group multiplication. In other words, the extroverted were no more effective in leading and multiplying a small group.

I was surprised by this finding. Before the survey, I thought those with more dynamic personalities would be more effective in leading and multiplying groups. However, the survey showed that the timid were just as effective in small group multiplication. Why? My theory is that introverted, timid people listen more rather than doing all the talking. Effective small groups focus on making disciples who make disciples rather than depending on one person.

This insight should encourage small group leaders to allow God to use the personality he has given. Great small group leaders depend on Jesus to provide them with the strength and power to guide the group. Jesus, not personality, makes small group leaders fruitful.

Giftedness

Before administrating this survey, I read that David Cho, pastor of the largest church in the history of Christianity, believed that those who could multiply a group had the gift of evangelism. I expected to confirm Cho's thinking. But we found the opposite. We discovered that the leader's particular gift did not correlate with whether the leader could multiply the small group.

The leaders listed various gifts (e.g., mercy, teaching, helps, leadership, and evangelism). The survey showed that those with the gift of mercy were just as effective as those with the gift of evangelism or leadership. One gift did not stand out as being more important.

Effective small group leaders mobilize all the gifts present in the group rather than depend on their own. Everyone has something to contribute to the overall purpose of making disciples who make disciples.

Small group leaders should not make the mistake of thinking that one gift is needed to facilitate and multiply the group. Trust the Spirit of God and identify the gifts of every member in the small group.

Education

Many doubt that they are qualified to lead a small group because they lack higher-level education. Our survey of 700 small group leaders showed a great range of levels of education, all the way from less than a sixth-grade education to the Ph.D. level. Yet, there was no correlation between education and multiplication.

The *tendency,* in fact, was that those with less education multiplied their groups more frequently than those with more education, although the correlation wasn't statistically significant enough to highlight this point.

We come back to this important point: Jesus is the one who gives wisdom and anointing to the leader, not education. The danger of highly educated people is to depend on their knowledge rather than Jesus Christ. Instead, they must trust Jesus and him alone to give grace to effectively mobilize the entire group in the process of making disciples who make disciples that results in multiplication.

Gender of the Leader

Do males multiply groups more than females? Vice-versa? The survey showed no correlation between small group multiplication and gender. Interestingly, 70% of the small group leaders in David Cho's church, Yoido Full Gospel Church, are female.

Conclusion

What I've shared in this lesson is just a sample of the findings from the survey. These factors and others point to one thing: Spirit-filled leaders more frequently multiply their small groups.

Scripture tells us that in our weakness, Jesus is made strong (1 Corinthians 12:9). John 15:1-5 reminds us that Jesus is the vine and that we are the branches. If we depend on him, we will bring forth much fruit. He will give us the victory.

Reflection Questions

What is the central truth that you have learned from this lesson?

How did this lesson encourage you in your small group leadership?

What errors did the findings of Comiskey's survey correct in your thinking of small group leadership?

What will you do differently because of these findings?

Suggested resources

Books

- *chapter 3 of Home Cell Group Explosion: How Your Small Group Can Grow and Multiply*
- *Lesson 4 of Lead: Guide a Small Group to Experience Christ*

Dissertation Chapter 9: Cell Multiplication

Dissertation Chapter 10: Recommendations, summary, conclusions

Multiplication Statistics (details on results of the Ph.D. statistical study)

Everyone Can Lead: Seeing Everyone as a Potential Leader

Everyone Can Lead: The Perfect Leader Doesn't Exist

Everyone Can Lead: Don't Overlook Anyone

Everyone a Potential Cell Leader

Seeing Everyone as a Disciple-maker (not "leader")

Download this PowerPoint

Joel Comiskey's PowerPoint on this lesson:

https://www.dropbox.com/s/e0gvjatsnmzs0hk/ lesson13-anyoneCanLead.pptx?dl=0

Prayer — a key factor in the multiplication of Groups

WATCH THIS VIDEO ▶

https://youtu.be/Y-9AKf9zr9k

I believe that anyone can effectively lead a small group and even multiply it. Fruitful small leadership does not depend on personality, a specific gift, education, or gender. However, in our study of 700 small group leaders in eight countries, we did notice one crucial factor that correlated precisely with multiplication: prayer.

Prayer stood out as having a direct relationship with whether the leader could multiply the small group. Here's the question we asked, "How much time do you spend in daily devotions? (e.g., prayer, Bible reading, etc.)." The question was clear and upfront. Those who took the survey knew we were referring to the devotional time or the quiet time.

We received a wide range of answers. Notice the percentages of spending time with Jesus among the 700 cell leaders:

Time spent in Devotions	Percentage of those questioned
0-15 minutes	11.7%
15-30 minutes	33.2%
30 minutes to 1 hour	33.8%
1 to 1 ½ hours	7.6%
1 ½ hours +	13.7%

As we analyzed the data, we noticed a clear correlation between time spent with God and whether the leader could multiply their cell group.

The survey did not explain why time spent with God correlated to small group multiplication, but we can surmise the answer. Those leaders who were spending daily quiet time were more sensitive to the voice of the Spirit. They heard from God about their small group. God showed them now to encourage the timid and redirect the conversation from the talker. Jesus filled them and gave them insight about how to make disciples who make disciples. The result was small group multiplication.

Jesus said in Matthew 6:6, "But when you pray, go into your room, close the door and pray to your Father, who is unseen. Then your Father, who sees what is done in secret, will reward you." Notice that Jesus says "when." He is talking about a specific time of prayer. Yes, we need to pray continually throughout the day (1 Thessalonians 5:16), but Jesus also tells us to set a specific time for concentrated prayer.

Many have used the phrase a *quiet time* or *devotional time* to describe this daily set time. While it's important to pray all the time, we can concentrate on God and his Word when we set a specific, daily time. God can fill us at any time, but he knows that we are ready, waiting, and prepared during our set time with him.

Notice that Jesus tells us to close the door in Matthew 6:6. What does Christ mean? He is referring to shutting out the noise and the distractions. When we pray during the day, we often face noisy interruptions. Personal devotional time allows us to *shut the door* to those things that distract us. We can concentrate on Jesus and his Word.

Jesus tells us that the Father who sees in secret will openly reward those who seek him in private. This *reward* was what I discovered in the study of 700 small group leaders. The heavenly Father was helping those leaders who spent time with him to multiply their groups. He was giving them strength and wisdom to do it.

Small group leadership can be discouraging. Those invited often fail to show up. Or maybe the leader is having a bad day. And, of course, the enemy of our souls, Satan, and his demons, attack the small group leaders and try to discourage them to the point of quitting the groups. Paul says, "For our struggle is not against flesh and blood, but against the rulers, against the authorities, against the powers of this dark world and against the spiritual forces of evil in the heavenly realms" (Ephesians 6:12).

Those leaders who spent specific time with the Father each day were encouraged to press ahead, even in the face of discouragement. When they felt depleted and discouraged, they returned to the God of the universe who refreshed them and gave them strength.

As I do seminars worldwide, I constantly tell small group leaders to spend daily time with God. I know how critical it is to set a daily time to seek the Father and receive his grace and mercy. I have two books on this topic, *An Appointment with the King* and *Grow: Grow: Deepen Your Relationship with Christ*. Both books focus on how to have a daily quiet time.

Another related survey question was how often the leader prayed for the members. Frequency in praying for members correlated with cell group effectiveness and multiplication. Some leaders didn't pray for the members, while some prayed occasionally. Yet, those leaders who prayed daily for their small group members were far more likely to multiply their groups.

The research didn't tell us why this is true, but we can surmise that the leaders who prayed continually for their members developed a spiritual authority and relationship. When the leaders were present with the members, they were able to minister more effectively. Paul said to the Colossian believers, "For though I am absent from you in body, I am present with you in spirit and delight to see how disciplined you are and how firm your faith in Christ is" (Colossians 2:5). Paul was present with them through prayer.

Leader, take the time to pray daily for those in the group. As you do, you will increase your authority and effectiveness. God will give you the grace to lead and multiply your small group. Remember that effective small group leadership comes from Jesus.

He's the one who anoints, guides, and gives fruit. As leaders spend time with him, Jesus will make them fruitful, glorify the Father's name, and fill the earth with disciples who make disciples for his glory.

Reflection Questions

What is the primary truth that you have learned from this lesson?

How did this lesson encourage you in your small group leadership?

How are you doing in personal devotions? What will you do differently because of this lesson?

Suggested resources

Books

- *An Appointment with the King: Ideas for Jump-Starting Your Devotional Life*
- *Grow: Deepen Your Relationship with Christ*
- *Chapter 3 of Home Cell Group Explosion: How Your Small Group Can Grow and Multiply*
- *Chapter 1 of How to Lead a Great Cell Group So People Want to Come Back*

Internet articles (available at
www.joelcomiskeygroup.com/resources)

> *Daily Soul Care for Cell Leaders*
> *Spending Time with Jesus*
> *Starting the Year Right with Jesus*
> *Hindrances to Spending Time with Jesus*
> *Prayer: We Need the Total Solution*
> *Prayer: Types of Prayer in the Cell Church*
> *Prayer: Hindrances and Suggestions to Overcome*
> *Them*
> *Prayer: How to Sustain Prayer*

Download this PowerPoint

Joel Comiskey's PowerPoint on this lesson:

https://www.dropbox.com/s/e128sxqez3yv55v/
lesson14-prayerKeyFactor.pptx?dl=0

Diligence — a Key Factor in Small Group Multiplication

WATCH THIS VIDEO ▶

https://youtu.be/Hofm_zGFXk8

W hen thinking of the factors that correlate with effective small group leadership, prayer is essential. But are there other important factors? In our study of 700 small group leaders in eight countries, we noticed various correlations between multiplication and leadership effectiveness, such as setting goals for the group, outside meetings, and building the team. But these additional reasons for multiplication could be summed up in the word *diligence.*

One of my professors at Fuller Seminary, who helped analyze the findings of the 700 cell leaders, said, "Joel, it looks like what you found in your research is that those who pray and work hard multiply their small groups." I thought, "Is that all I discovered. I paid all this money to discover that?" Often God uses simple formulas, ones that we might think are not sophisticated enough. The simple finding was that those leaders who prayed often and worked diligently could multiply their small groups.

In Romans 12:8, Paul connects diligence with leadership. He says, "if it is to encourage, then give encouragement; if it is giving, then give generously; *if it is to lead, do it diligently;* if it is to show mercy, do it cheerfully." Leadership and diligence go together.

The Greek word for diligence is *spoudé.* It means *quick movement in the interest of a person or cause.* We can see *spoudé* used in several Bible verses like 2 Timothy 2:15 says, "Do your best [*spoude*] to present yourself to God as one approved, a worker who does not need to be ashamed and who correctly handles the word of truth." We have three words in English, but there's only one word in Greek: *spoudé.*

Another example is Hebrew 4:11, "Let us, therefore, make every effort [*spoudé*] to enter that rest, so that no one will perish by following their example of disobedience."

Those small group leaders who prayed and worked hard could find solutions for their group and effectively made disciples who made other disciples. In other words, fruitful small group leaders didn't give up. When they hit a brick wall, they prayed and asked God how to find a way around it or over it. God helped them to keep pressing ahead despite the obstacles.

I remember one leader saying to me, "Joel, I don't have the gift of making phone calls." I wanted to tell him, "who has the gift of making phone calls?" You do it. You just pick up the phone and say, "Nancy, I noticed that you weren't in the group last night. How can I pray for you?"

Nike has made famous the slogan, *just do it*. And this is so true of fruitful small group leaders. They just do it. If they invite five people and no one shows up, they continue to invite others. If they become discouraged, as all small group leaders do, they go back to Jesus in prayer and ask him to fill them with the Holy Spirit.

If they invite people to a barbeque, and it doesn't work, they might show a Christian movie and invite people to watch it, hold a special outreach to the poor, or invite people to a sports event. The study revealed that there was no secret formula. No magic bullet. Those who were fruitful in small group ministry found a way to make it work.

Thomas Edison invented the light bulb, but in the process, he failed 2000 times. One reporter said to him, "Didn't you feel like a failure?" He said that he was simply 2000 steps closer to inventing the light bulb. Fruitful small group leaders go back to their quiet time when they're ready to give up. They ask Jesus for special encouragement. *Spoudé.*

I remember visiting a famous small group-based church in Louisiana. The group was holding a multiplication party, complete with a birthday cake to celebrate the new birth. The leader was so excited and proud because he was about to multiply his group. The supervisor was present, along with the zone pastor. We had an excellent barbeque that night, southern style: gumbo, ribs, and the whole works.

But when only dirty dishes were in the sink, and everyone was gone, I approached the small group leader and said, "What did you do to arrive at this point of multiplication?" He told me, "Joel, I was about to close this group nine months ago, but I continued to pray and invite people. A young person came to the group, received Jesus, and began to invite all his friends. Here we are ready to multiply."

I didn't know it then, but now I know that the word was *spoudé*. This leader didn't give up. He kept pressing on until he multiplied his group. And that's the same truth that God wants us to understand today: *spoudé*. Prayer and spoudé. Jesus will help you lead and multiply your group. Just remember; prayer and spoudé.

Reflection Questions

What is the central truth that you have learned from this lesson?
How does diligence connect with prayer?
In what area do you need to be more diligent in your small group leadership?

Suggested resources

Books

- *Chapter 5 of Leadership Explosion: Multiplying Cell Leaders for the Harvest*
- *Chapter 6 of Lead: Guide a Small Group to Experience Christ*

**Internet articles (available at
www.joelcomiskeygroup.com/resources)**

> *Spoudé (diligence): the Key to Effective Cell
>   Leadership*
> *Don't Give Up (whether you're a cell leader or
>   church planter)*

Download this PowerPoint

Joel Comiskey's PowerPoint on this lesson:

*https://www.dropbox.com/s/0ezcjajeegr2r54/
lesson15-diligenceKeyFactor.pptx?dl=0*

Practices of Effective Small Group Leaders

WATCH THIS VIDEO ▶

https://youtu.be/6ZZWiZ2uogA

We know that prayer and diligence corresponded with small group multiplication. Our study of 700 small group leaders in 8 countries discovered that those leaders who prayed and worked hard could multiply their groups more frequently.

Yet, what does it mean to work hard? Or, more specifically, in what areas should the leader practice diligence? The study pointed to at least three areas: community, outreach, and developing new leaders.

Community

Those groups that had deeper community also multiplied more rapidly. We measured this by outside meetings: the frequency of time spent together outside the group. Those groups that spent more time together were also groups that were likely to multiply.

Jesus and the New Testament writers talk a lot about practicing the one-anothers of Scripture: loving one another, serving one another, building up one another, and so forth. The small group is the perfect place to practice these truths. And in fact, this was the atmosphere in which the early church was born. Intimacy established in the small group should not just stay inside the group. It also must flourish outside the group as the members grow deeper with each other.

The small group leader doesn't need to develop all the relationships. I was in one group in which the leader said, "Joel, I don't know if I can continue to lead the group. I just don't have the time to develop all the relationships." I replied, "God isn't calling you to develop all the relationships. He wants you to encourage the others to develop relationships with each other." Members can grow in their relationships by going out to coffee together, gathering in accountability groups, hang-out after church, and so forth. Healthy, loving groups multiply. My book *Relational Disciple* talks about building relationships in the group.

Evangelism

The most effective groups grow in evangelism and community—not one or the other. The best groups have both. They are concerned about intimacy among the members, but they also evangelize those who didn't know Jesus.

Those groups in my study which invited others to the group were far more likely to multiply their groups. Members must know that the group's purpose is to go beyond close fellowship and reach those who don't know Jesus. As the group does reach out, each member will grow spiritually, and the group will also have closer unity. It's like soldiers who go to battle together. They have a common objective of defeating the enemy, but they also grow in unity and camaraderie as a result.

When Jesus told his disciples that he would make them *fishers of men* (Matthew 4:19), he was talking about group fishing, using a net rather than an individual fishing pole. Cell evangelism is primarily a group activity as opposed to an individual one. The group plans the outreach and reaps the fruit together. My book *Share* talks about evangelism in general but also emphasizes the group aspect of evangelism.

Developing New Leaders

Scripture tells us in Matthew 9 that Jesus had compassion as he looked at the multitude. He then told his disciples, "The harvest is plentiful, but the workers are few. Ask the Lord of the harvest, therefore, to send out workers into his harvest field." (Matthew 9:37-38).

Jesus tells us that one of the primary reasons for not reaping the harvest is the lack of laborers. Small groups are a wonderful place to develop future laborers and leaders. Jesus himself had a small group and prepared the disciples who would change the world in the small group. The early church met in homes and developed leadership from those homes.

I love the illustration of Peter walking to Jesus on the water (Matthew 14:22-33). Peter wanted to come to Jesus on the water, and Jesus invited him to come. Jesus encouraged him to experiment. Peter sank in doubt, but Jesus was there to rescue him. And Jesus loves it when we step out by faith and come to him.

Effective small group leaders encourage the members to participate in each aspect of the small group—even if they fail in the process. The best way to learn is through experience and failure. The best leaders encourage the members to use their muscles and grow in the process. They also should encourage the members to take the church-wide equipping to prepare them to be future leaders.

Reflection Questions

What is the primary truth that you have learned from this lesson?

Of the three practices discussed in this lesson, which one do you need to work on the most?

How are you allowing the members to step out and even fail in your group?

Suggested resources

Books

- Chapter 1-4, 7-14 of *Leadership Explosion: Multiplying Cell Leaders for the Harvest*
- Chapter 6 of *Home Cell Group Explosion: How Your Small Group Can Grow and Multiply*

Internet articles (available at www.joelcomiskeygroup.com/resources)

The Leader Driven Church
Releasing Leaders for the Harvest
Making Yourself Dispensable
From Conversion to Baptism
Developing Leaders from Within: Introduction
Developing Leaders from Within: Developing Missionaries and Church Planters
Developing Leaders from Within: Expanding Leadership
Developing Leaders from Within: Don't Short-Change the Leadership
Making Disciples: The Purpose of Small Groups
From Leader to Disciple-maker
Key Principle: Making Disciples who Make Disciples
How to Define a Disciple in the Cell Church (D1-4)

*Maturing by Taking the Next Step in Cell
Ministry*
*Seeing Everyone as a Disciple-maker (not
"leader")*
Making Disciples Like Jesus
Discipleship Is the Main Thing

Download this PowerPoint

Joel Comiskey's PowerPoint on this lesson:

*https://www.dropbox.com/s/nhhfh558j9p963j/
lesson16-practicesMultiplication.
pptx?dl=0*

Groups that Thrive — Empowerment and Community

WATCH THIS VIDEO ▶

https://youtu.be/6ZZWiZ2uogA

Misconceptions are common in small group ministry. For example, most books on small group ministry assume that the leader is the key behind thriving groups. Or we might think that those groups which excel in community are not highly effective in evangelism.

Jim Egli and I wanted to expel some of the small group myths, so we polled 1800 leaders in four different countries: the USA, Brazil, Latin America, and China to discover what made groups thrive. We came up with eight special surprises, which we highlight in our book *Groups that Thrive*.

Although we talk about eight surprises in the book, I'll highlight two of them in this lesson: empowerment of the members and the relationship between community and evangelism.

Regarding the empowerment of the members, we discovered that the best groups were the ones in which the members took ownership of the group. Groups were far more effective in multiplication when the members thought of the group as "their group" rather than the leader's group. We also found that groups in which people were involved were far more likely to reach out and invite new members.

Negatively, the unhealthiest groups were those in which the leader tried to do everything. One negative correlation in our study was when the leader agreed with the statement, "I like to do everything myself." Those groups were the unhealthiest in every category.

The best thing the leader can do is empower the members to take ownership in the small group. The key is to help change the member's thinking from the "leader's group" to "our group." How can the leader do this? By giving the members responsibilities in the group each time. Allow Joe to lead the prayer time, ask Mary to lead worship, and John to lead the lesson.

The best groups rotate among the leadership team to lead the different aspects of the group. The best leaders prepare others, offer plenty of encouragement with some suggestions, and allow members to *fail forward.* Your group will come to life as a result.

The same is true for evangelism and outreach. Those groups which felt ownership were more effective in reaching out. The leader is key to creating that atmosphere. Remember the word *facilitate.* Facilitate has to do with empowering and making it easy for others to participate.

Christ's original small group was dynamic. The disciples participated, asked questions, and practiced on-the-job training. Jesus knew that this is how people grow, and he modeled it for the ages to come.

Another surprise was how community interacted with evangelism. We discovered that those groups which experienced intimate community were also more effective in reaching out. The connection between community and evangelism surprised me. For a long time, I thought that if a group became too intimate, it would stagnate and lose its effectiveness.

Our study confirmed that groups with more intimacy were also more effective in multiplication and keeping their members.

I must admit that I've multiplied groups too rapidly in the past, thinking that I needed to reproduce after a specific period. Because I didn't fully prepare the next leader or group members, those groups ended up dying. I have since learned to prioritize community and member development, knowing that thriving small groups are intimate groups.

I often highlight my wife Celyce as an example of someone who has multiplied many healthy groups. I've noticed that Celyce concentrates on relationships and love among the members. Her groups multiplied naturally.

Jim Egli and I analyzed the impact of food in the group and found that food correlated with thriving, healthy small groups. Now, this does not mean that each group needs to have a full meal each week. We found that it's best to create variety. For example, a group might have a full dinner together followed by a light snack.

Jesus wants to give us thriving small groups that make disciples who make disciples for his glory.

Reflection Questions

What is the main truth that you have learned from
this lesson?

Of the three practices discussed in this lesson, which
one do you need to work on the most?

How are you allowing the members to step out and
even fail in your group?

Suggested resources

Books

- *Chapters 1-4 of Groups that Thrive: 8
  Surprising Discoveries About Life-Giving
  Small Groups*

Internet articles (available at
www.joelcomiskeygroup.com/resources)

Discipleship through Community
Transformed by the One Anothers of Scripture
Why Community is Important to God
Relational Discipleship
The Church as a Family
My Journey into Cell Community
The Power of Cell Community during Crisis
Community that Transforms

Myth: Don't Get Too Close to People in the Group
Community is a Good Thing
More than Evangelism: The Case for Community
Family: The Family of God and Cell Ministry
Family: The Key Image of Scripture
Family: Group Orientation of Scripture
Family: Strengthening the Family Today

Download this PowerPoint

Joel Comiskey's PowerPoint on this lesson:

*https://www.dropbox.com/s/3utvpwtj8pgti9v/
    lesson17-thriveEmpowermentCommunity.
    pptx?dl=0*

Groups that Thrive — Transparency and Worship

WATCH THIS VIDEO ▶

https://youtu.be/eNNyeiJWGo4

In one group, I asked each member to invite a friend. One of the members said in front of everyone, "Joel, I'm here because I want to share what's going on in my life, and I don't want new people to be in the group." I was shocked by her words, but I did appreciate her honesty. The following week I talked to her privately, saying that while we wanted to go deeper and grow in intimacy, we also wanted to reach out to new people. I explained to her that the DNA of our group was evangelism and deep community. But is this possible?

Transparent sharing and evangelism

Even though I believe in both aspects of group life, I still didn't know if inviting new people hindered open sharing. Jim Egli and I had the chance to test the correlation between transparency and evangelism statistically. We polled 1800 small group leaders in four language groups: Mandarin (China), Spanish (Latin America), Portuguese (Brazil), and English (North America).

We asked several questions about the level of open sharing in the group and whether the group members felt the liberty to share their struggles. We then compared what we found with groups reaching out versus closed groups.

We discovered that small groups that were actively reaching non-Christians also shared more deeply and intimately. In other words, the closed, non-evangelizing groups were less intimate!

The statistics didn't tell us why this was so. Yet, I can surmise that those groups which were more transparent were also more attractive to Non-Christians. The reality is that Christians are not perfect—just forgiven. They are like beggars telling other beggars where to get bread.

In his book *Small Group Evangelism*, Richard Peace talks about the power of transparent sharing to attract non-Christians. He believes that the best group evangelism involves honest sharing as non-Christians realize that believers have everyday struggles. They witness that believers place their difficulties at the foot of the cross. Evangelism becomes an ongoing process, and when the unbeliever receives Jesus, they have a family in which they can journey and grow.

In one of the groups I led, a particular member felt the liberty to share her doubts about "religion." We all focused on open sharing, so she felt the freedom to do the same. The rest of the group just listened and loved her. One evening we played .15 minutes of the Jesus video film, and before it finished, she cried out, "I'm confused." The rest of the group just loved her, and two weeks later, she received Jesus as her Lord and Savior. She continued to attend the group, which had become her family. She went through the equipping and eventually became a small group leader.

Worship and Evangelism

What about worship in the small group? Does worship hinder evangelism and outreach? We asked the leaders whether they included worship singing in their small group. We discovered that those groups that included worship were also more effective in reaching non-believers.

Our study focused on worship singing, but worship also includes prayer, Scripture reading, and so forth.

What we discovered is that non-Christians want to experience God. They need God's touch, and that is why they are in the group. We must not hide God from them because we are afraid we might offend them. Worship is part of that experience.

This study has helped me to prioritize small group worship. I now realize that worship not only pleases God and edifies believers, but non-Christians are also attracted to worship. Jesus said, "If I'm lifted up, I'll draw all men to myself" (John 12:32). Jesus refers to his death on the cross, but we can apply his words to the small group. When we exalt Jesus, he draws people to himself.

Today, it's easier than ever to worship in a small group because of the many varied resources available. We can invite Hillsong into our small groups via YouTube. I encourage leaders to ensure that new-comers can see the words on a screen or printed out sheets.

I've highlighted two surprises in this lesson, but we discuss all eight of them in the book *Groups that Thrive*. Jesus wants to help your group to thrive.

Reflection Questions

What is the central truth that you have learned from this lesson?

How has your group prioritized worship? How has this lesson encouraged you to prioritize worship in your small group?

What have you discovered about evangelism and transparent sharing in your group? How did this lesson change your thinking?

Suggested Resources

Books

- *Chapters 5-8 of Groups that Thrive: 8 Surprising Discoveries About Life-Giving Small Groups*

Transparency: Don't Hide Behind Curriculum
Transparency in the Cell Group
Transparency Killers
Transparency: Lead the Way
God-Sensitive Small Groups
Worship Singing: Is it Worth Including in the Cell?
Worship in the Cell Group
People Want to Experience God in the Cell
How God's Healing Power Can Transform the Cell Group

Download this PowerPoint

Joel Comiskey's PowerPoint on this lesson:

https://www.dropbox.com/s/u8vr59kwf5igs85/ lesson18-thriveTransparencyWorship. pptx?dl=0

www.ingramcontent.com/pod-product-compliance
Lightning Source LLC
LaVergne TN
LVHW051418080426
835508LV00022B/3140